A Day in the Life of an American Bullfrog

Julie Murray

Abdo Kids Junior
is an Imprint of Abdo Kids
abdobooks.com

Abdo
A DAY IN THE LIFE
OF AN ANIMAL
Kids

abdobooks.com

Published by Abdo Kids, a division of ABDO, P.O. Box 398166, Minneapolis, Minnesota 55439.

Printed in the United States of America, North Mankato, Minnesota.

102025

012026

Photo Credits: AdobeStock, Alamy, Getty Images, Science Source, Shutterstock

Production Contributors: Teddy Borth, Jennie Forsberg, Grace Hansen

Design Contributors: Candice Keimig, Pakou Moua

Library of Congress Control Number: 2025936386

Publisher's Cataloging-in-Publication Data

Names: Murray, Julie, author.

Title: A day in the life of an American bullfrog / by Julie Murray

Description: Minneapolis, Minnesota : Abdo Kids, 2026 | Series: A day in the life of an animal | Includes online resources and index.

Identifiers: ISBN 9798384907329 (lib. bdg.) | ISBN 9798384908029 (ebook) | ISBN 9798384908371 (read-to-me ebook)

Subjects: LCSH: American bull frog--Juvenile literature. | Frogs--Juvenile literature. | Amphibians—Juvenile literature. | Amphibians--Behavior--Juvenile literature. | Animal behavior--Juvenile literature. | Herpetology--Juvenile literature.

Classification: DDC 597.89--dc23

Table of Contents

An American Bullfrog's Day

The sun is up! The American bullfrog **basks** in its warmth.

It rests near the edge of the pond.

It swims in the water.

It uses its **webbed** feet.

The sun goes down.
The frog begins to
make noise.

It makes loud croaking sounds.

It sits and waits for **prey**.

It sees an insect.

It uses its strong back legs.

It leaps forward.

It opens its mouth.

It catches the **prey**.

It swallows it whole.

The frog rests again.

It waits for another meal.

American Bullfrog Facts

Can live 7 to 10 years in the wild

Can weigh up to 3 pounds (1.4 kg)

Native to parts of North America

Usually 6 to 8 (15.2–20.3 cm) inches in length

Glossary

bask
to lie in a warm, calm place.

prey
an animal that is hunted by other animals for food.

webbed
joined by thin skin.

Index

Visit **abdokids.com** to access crafts, games, videos, and more!

Use Abdo Kids code **AAK7329** or scan this QR code!